D0423192

MARK RUTLAND

Word of Life Series

HOLINESS
The Perfect Word
to Imperfect People

HOLINESS by Mark Rutland
Published by Creation House
A Strang Company
600 Rinehart Road
Lake Mary, Florida 32746
www.creationhouse.com

All Scripture quotations are from the King James Version of the Bible.

Cover design by Rachel Campbell

Library of Congress Control Number: 2004117102
International Standard Book Number: 1-59185-788-0

05 06 07 08 09 — 987654321
Printed in the United States of America

In Loving Memory

of

Dr. Tommy Tyson
A true Israelite in whom there was no guile

Acknowledgments

$\mathcal{A}$T ONE of Southeastern University's marvelous theatrical productions, a rogue serious thought invaded the delightful escapism of the moment. I began to contemplate all that went on behind the majestically talented performers on the stage. Set design, costume and prop management, lighting, and sound were all perfect yet those responsible were cloaked in anonymity. I thought of all the moms who drove to countless music lessons, dads who paid for the lessons, and teachers long forgotten who cracked open the tough nut of music for unpromising beginners. There was no way to bring them on stage for a bow but at least for a moment by one in that audience they were remembered.

Pause if you will and think kindly of those whose names are not on this book yet whose contributions to it were invaluable. Think of my fifth grade teacher who encouraged my dream of writing, of my wife who listens to me read my manuscripts aloud and praises them extravagantly, and of those silent servants who type, correct, and retype until a finished work evolves. Think of my children who actually read and claim to enjoy my books, of my son who keeps demanding more, and of my friend Tommy Tyson who taught me that thinking was permissible for believers.

All on stage for a bow! May they be rewarded in public who have labored in silence.

Table of Contents

1 More Than a Masquerade...................... *1*

2 Beyond a Broken God...........................*15*

3 Inside Out...*29*

4 The Finger of God *50*

5 Shards on the Altar...............................*72*

Chapter 1

More Than a Masquerade

A YOUNG MAN awaiting a bus was joined on the bus stop bench by a nun. Seeing no one near enough to hear him, he leaned close and whispered to the nun.

"Sister, forgive me, but I have always had a fantasy of kissing a nun. Please don't be offended, but would you let me give you a quick kiss on the cheek?"

Far from being offended, the nun answered in a gentle tone, "I will let you kiss me on two conditions. You must be a Catholic, and you must be single."

"This is my lucky day," he beamed. "I happen to be Catholic, and I'm single."

With that he eagerly kissed her on the cheek. Then he laughed at her. "Sister, the joke is on you. I'm married, and I'm a Baptist."

"No," the nun answered, "the joke's on you. My name is Kevin, and I'm on my way to a costume party."

We expend untold kilowatts of emotional,

relational, and spiritual energy trying to convince each other that we are other than we are. The modern church is the Disneyland of denial and deception. Our masks are so winsome and our religiosity so convincing that the game of "fool me—fool you" has all too often turned the community of faith into a masquerade ball for the willingly deluded.

In the process, one word, one great truth, has been virtually forgotten. Denounced by some as an irrelevant antique and counterfeited by those in religious costumes, this great truth awaits a fresh rediscovery by hungry postmodernists.

Nestled among my funnier memories is the picture of a small, frame church squatting unpretentiously beside the loop around a certain southern city. Even to this day I chuckle at the thought of its name: "The Bypass Holiness Church." Terrific, isn't it? I have known a lot of churches that wanted to bypass holiness, but I have seldom seen one advertise it so brazenly.

Bypassing holiness is certainly not new. The word *holiness* itself has passed in and out of vogue throughout the more than two thousand years of church history. Sometimes holiness almost disappears under the scorn of a contemporary religious culture that finds the word, if not the reality, awkward and embarrassing. The word has been abused, despised, and relegated to history's hall of antiques, but as long as there is a Bible anywhere in the world, it will never disappear.

The problem is that postmodernists, both inside and outside the church, have no idea what *holiness* means. Hijacked by neo-Pharisees, mocked by postmodern liberals, and all too often ignored by contemporary pulpits, holiness must be unearthed, revived, and freshly articulated. The word needs no redefinition; indeed, it resists any such effort. What is needed, desperately needed, is a new wave of creative expression in print and pulpit. Holiness has never gone anywhere. It never will. It is, however, high time to talk about it again, believe in it again, and seek it again.

What happens to words? How did *gay* come to mean homosexual, for example? Who made "bad to the bone" a compliment? The theft, or loss, of a perfectly good word is always lamentable. People do not think in pictures or concepts but in words. When a society's vocabulary shrinks or is corrupted, its ability to think in entire areas of life goes missing. Regardless of which of a culture's rooms go dark, the damage is real and terrible. That some of the vocabulary now being squandered is biblical speaks to the postmodern inability to think clearly about God. In other words, when our God-language goes down the drain, informed, thoughtful faith in God goes with it.

The Mad Hatter told Alice that when he used a word, it meant whatever he wanted it to mean. When that becomes the creed of a culture, meaninglessness will follow. If everything means everything, then nothing means anything. Words must mean what they mean. Otherwise men will not mean what they say or say what they mean.

What we believe to be true about God, about who He is and what He wants, becomes warped, terrifyingly twisted, when we suffer the theft of the words we use to think of Him. Words like *grace*, *judgment*, and *redemption* have to mean things, and we have to know what they mean or their benefit in our lives may never be received. How will men seek and have confidence in blessings that have never been explained or meaningfully proffered?

Among all the battered words of transcendent

biblical truth, among all the lost and forgotten words of Scripture rejected by the postmodern church and world, one has taken the worst beating. The testimony of its eternal worth and weight is the vehemence with which it has been ill-treated. Not simply laid aside, but cast out, this one word, rediscovered, has the power to change a world in desperate need of change.

Driving through a small, southern town I saw another church sign I'll never forget. Rudely hand painted, it boasted a screaming red arrow pointing down a side street. Above that scarlet arrow, printed irregularly in white, were six memorable words: *Holey Ghost Revival Now in Progress.*

It occurred to me in that moment that the greatest impediment to a modern move of God may lie in our spelling. *Holey* means full of holes. Holey is your socks, not your God. Holey is, in fact, the exact opposite of *holy.*

Holiness means perfect, entire, wanting nothing for completion. *Holy* means nothing missing and nothing extra. Incomplete and full of lies, a politician's answers are holey, not holy. With the truth missing and with deceptions present, his answers lack what they ought to have and have what they should not. Unholy answers are holey indeed.

Imagine a circle, a perfect circle, equidistant from the center at every point on a circumference. It satisfies the definition of "circle-ness" in every way. It is a holy circle, not morally, of course, but by definition. Now take your mental eraser and rub out part of the circumference. Now it's holey. Take your imaginary chalk and fill in the gap, not along the correct circumference, but with a corkscrew design. Now the circle is no circle at all, but something else, some undefined geometric counterfeit of a near-circle. Circle? Close but no cigar. The "circle" with holes in its perimeter is holey, and the one with uncircle-like matter on its border is corrupted by the extra-definitional nonsense added to its edge. Neither are circles.

When I was in undergraduate school, I took a relatively blasphemous course called philosophy. My professor, I'll call him Dr. Johnson, was an atheist—an aggressive and evangelistic atheist. Not content to go to hell alone, he intended that we should all go with him. If he found out any of his students were Christians, he would lower the guns to deck level and load with grape shot. One morning it was my turn.

"Stand up, Mr. Rutland. I understand you are a Christian."

"Yes, Dr. Johnson, I am." I was ferociously determined to make a witness to him and the class.

"Then you must believe in God."

"Yes, of course, Dr. Johnson. It is impossible to be a Christian without a belief in God."

"I thought so. Let me ask you something. Can your God do everything?"

Aha! I thought. This was the perfect opening to testify boldly to God's greatness. Raising my right hand for dramatic effect, I gave him the obvious answer.

"Yes, sir, Dr. Johnson, God can do everything."

"Then riddle me this. Can God create a rock He cannot pick up?"

I was the dumbstruck and embarrassed prey at the mercy of a classroom full of hungry hyenas. He had me. If God could not make the rock, that violated the proposition. If He could make it and could not pick it up, that violated the proposition. I was publicly trapped by an experienced trapper of innocent freshmen, and there was nothing I could do. It was too late to escape, and I did not know how anyway. Full of youthful enthusiasm, my answer was an apologetics disaster exploited by a vicious atheist. I lost that day, but I needn't have. Dr. Johnson's question was the correct one, and it deserved a bold answer filled with wisdom as well as faith.

Now, all these years later, I know the right answer. I am one of those people who always thinks of clever answers too late. I have often considered going back to school and see if that turkey would try that philosophical bubble gum on me one more time.

"Can God do everything?" is the most important question of eternity, and it must be answered, but the answer is not yes. The answer is no. No, God cannot do everything. He cannot lie. He cannot sin. He cannot will, think, or speak in contradiction to His own nature. He is more surely bound than a galley slave, but not by any limitation on His power. He is all-powerful, to be sure. The limitation is in His character. God can never be other than what He is. God cannot quit being God. There are no holes in God. There is nothing missing that would make Him more God than He is. Likewise, there is nothing in God, which, drained off, would purify His

Godness. God is holy, not holey, and His holiness is the hope of mankind.

I once knew a Chinese lady, quite an elderly old girl, whose childhood in a pre-communist, pagan household interested me a great deal. When a healthy baby, preferably a boy, was born into a home, it produced quite a fascinating bit of theater. The overjoyed parents would immediately hide both the infant and their delight. The father would then shoot fireworks or bang cymbals until, certain that he had the attention of the gods, he would revile them at the top of his lungs. Neighbors who came to see the new addition would energetically join in the charade. With a conspiratorial wink or a furtive handshake, friends would quickly and quietly acknowledge the little blessing, raise their voices, beat their breasts, and heap accusations on the gods.

"Woe to his house! Woe, woe!"

"This miserable excuse for a baby will never bring happiness to anyone."

"Why have you gods vexed this poor family with such a worthless child? How tragic is this day!"

Why all the theatrics? Because pagans understand the gods to be great, eternal human beings.

HOLINESS

A human magnified ten million times would be a formidable force. The problem, of course, is that such a huge human would also have huge human sins. Magnify the man; magnify his flaws. Imagine multiple gods, petty, envious children, lurking behind the clouds just waiting to crush happy people on earth like bugs. Seeing humans taking delight in a child, for example, they might well harm it. Better to feign unhappiness than to risk making such nasty creatures jealous. Such a religion is filled with fear and uncertainty because the gods of the pagans, like pagans themselves, are capricious and sinful. Such gods, able to do everything, are terrifying, indeed.

The God of Abraham is holy, and His holiness is the hope of humanity. Our God is not predictable, but He is dependable. We never need worry that God will be gracious one moment and envious the next. All-powerful, yet never a bully, God is happy when we are happy, blessed when we are blessed, and joyful at our abundance, which, after all, comes from Him.

A lady in one church told me that she steadfastly rejected talk of seeking God, or pressing in, or any other expression of drawing nigh. She, for one, was not taken in by such spurious admonitions. Rather than take dangerous risks, she proudly proclaimed she wanted to be a "C" Christian.

She straightforwardly admitted that she had done high school exactly the same way. If one does exceptionally well in school, she explained, people begin to expect things of you, and the bar simply gets higher and higher. On the other hand, she explained, do too poorly, and you flunk. She absolutely beamed telling me that she had graduated from high school with straight Cs, an academic balancing act to be sure.

Seeing that I was obviously impressed, she quickly made her theological application. If you are too bad, she soberly proclaimed, God will flunk you right into hell, and she definitely did not want to go to hell. By the same token, if you get very holy, she held, God will send you as a missionary to India, and she did not care to go to India, either. She, therefore, hoped to graduate to heaven with straight Cs.

No silly talk on my part about such nonsense as works righteousness could make a dent. She was determined to slip unnoticed into heaven, A-less and F-less, all smooth Cs. She had no more interest in knowing God than in rebelling against Him. What she did not want was to draw His attention. In that, she was more pagan than Christian.

Her unshakable commitment to Cs was rooted in a misunderstanding, quite a pagan misunderstanding actually, of who God is. She saw God as a magnified English teacher, grading strictly, hounding the bright into college, and chasing the not-so-clever into menial jobs. She had no thought of a holy God whose will for her life is good because He is good. Her pathetic confusion, far more serious than a mere epidermal misjudgment of "how God acts," sprang from a twisted concept of "who God is."

Far from being an isolated story, hers is a tragedy repeated with only slight variations in the lives of multiplied millions of sincere, but sincerely confused, Christians. These crippled children live shadowy lives of terror, fearful of a God they do not know. Without knowledge of the holiness of God, these people may well perish or at least huddle in cold darkness away from the light of God's holy love.

Out of the burning bush God spoke to Moses, calling him to the great life's work for which he had been raised up. It was a task of monumental proportion and must have been stunning to Moses. Of even greater significance today is Jehovah's self-declaration in that same conversation.

> And Moses said unto God, Behold, when I come unto the children of Israel, and shall say unto them, The God of your fathers hath sent me unto you; and they shall say to me, What is his name? what shall I say unto them?
>
> —EXODUS 3:13

It is quite provocative to note that Moses required no revelation to sway the might of Egypt. The demonstration of power was sufficient for Pharaoh. Moses knew it was the bound and backslidden people of God who needed a fresh revelation. The children of Israel had been so long in slavery amidst the pantheistic paganism of Egypt that they had lost sight of the true nature of a holy God. Moses could imagine their response: "We know the name of Isis and the name of Ra; when you speak of the God of our fathers, what is His name?"

It was in the light of such confusion that Moses asked God for revelation. Revival is not when pagans see the power of God, but when the people of God rediscover His nature and His name. Moses pled with God because His people were deeply confused. Four hundred years of bondage had done their work. Moses knew it was no use to tell the Hebrews that a burning bush had sent him. Moses wanted to know the name of God.

The answer of God was the revelation of His holiness. I AM that I AM. God announced to Moses, and to us, in no uncertain terms that He is true to Himself. He will never be one thing and then another. He is not a changeable Chinese dragon, blessing then cursing, depending on what mood He is in.

We are free from fear in the unshakable knowledge that God is none other or less than Himself. He is the present tense, unchanging, unchangeable ultimate reality of the universe, the ground of all truth and the hope of humanity. God is perfectly God.

Chapter 2
Beyond a Broken God

I ONCE HAD a great friend whom I loved dearly. Barry was a fine tennis player as well as a warm and witty companion. His wife, Martha, however, was demonized. She was as mean-hearted, mean-spirited, and cold-blooded a woman as ever lived.

Martha refused to condescend to such trite niceties as answering the phone with "Hello," "Good morning," or even "Barry and Martha's." Instead she would jerk the phone from its cradle as if personally insulted by its ring and loudly demand, "What?!" My request to speak to Barry usually earned me nothing but a tongue-lashing.

"He's home, but you can't speak to him. I'm tired of his dead-beat, tennis-bum friends calling up every time he has a few hours off. He's not going to play tennis *today*. We're going to work here at the house, and *anyway*, why don't you get married and settle down?"

This had a decided tendency to ruin my day. I

finally became unwilling to risk such harrowing encounters.

"Barry," I told my friend, "I love you, and I want to play tennis. But from now on *you* call *me*. My mama answers the phone, 'Hello.'"

If I could have hidden across the street to watch the house until Martha left, I might have called. But I would rather have missed tennis with my friend than risk hearing her shout, "What?!"

God alone knows how many multiplied millions of serious, church-trained folks are utterly paralyzed in their devotional access to God because they are not certain who will answer the phone when they dial heaven. If they could be certain to get Jesus on the phone, they would perhaps approach prayer with confidence. Afraid that God, the angry cop, might answer, they simply do not call. Many church-goers, while espousing Trinitarianism, are actually functioning Unitarians, serving the God Jesus and living in ignorant terror of the full Godhead. This is often reinforced at a cultural level in unfortunate and unintended ways.

Church in my childhood meant detached Sundays in the house of a God with multiple personalities. Sunday school was bright and warm.

A smiling, gray-haired teacher condescended to sit on a chair my size. She colored pictures with me and told me that Jesus loved me. How easy it was to believe! His blue-eyed, chestnut-haired countenance decorated our classroom wall. On our felt-board the teacher fearlessly put smiling children right on Jesus' lap. We celebrated Jesus' love for little children in general and for us personally with every song. At Easter the soft, warm bunny our teacher brought in a pasteboard carton seemed to have some vague connection to this misty-eyed Jesus and His love for children.

Church? Now *that* was a different matter! The staircase winding up from the basement Sunday school classrooms definitely led *away* from the festive presence of Jesus. Leaving my teacher singing, "Jesus Loves Me," I entered a somber oaken sanctuary where an organist belted out Bach like the phantom of the opera. Furthermore, the congregation was all adults. Every kid knows there is something spooky about a place where they don't allow babies. Finally, out came the preacher in a long black dress and the choir wearing their nightgowns. Gone was the friendly smile of my Sunday school teacher. The pastor, looking for all the world like a buzzard with a gland problem, bawled in phony voice that "Gawd is in His holy temple, let all the earth keep SILENCE before Him." Jesus, hardly mentioned again, was supplanted by "Gawd"! Imagine the shock for a child.

Hardly a setting designed to draw a child to the bosom of the Father, it more nearly scared the wits out of me. And what did it say about the Trinity? I knew that part of God, the nice part, the Sunday school part, Jesus, was on *my* side. Gawd the Father was obviously angry at the entire universe, and the Holy Spirit seemed to be window dressing, mentioned only in monotonous rituals and meaningless creeds.

In some of the churches of my adult life it appears reversed. All about Jesus, His mercy, His grace, His sacrifice, these churches seem to have forgotten the Father who is I AM. Others are apparently Holy Spirit churches, seldom mentioning either the Atonement or the Father, celebrating instead an almost exclusively pneumatological faith. Gifts, signs, and miracles witness to the Spirit's presence in Pentecostal power, but the wholeness of God's creative and redemptive nature seems emptied into the Spirit alone.

In some evangelical circles this fractured view

of the triune Godhead has likewise produced a fractured "gospel according to Pocahontas." Jesus is portrayed as saving us from God, an obvious extrapolation of the Jesus-loves-me-but-Gawd-is-ticked-off concept. Scripture, however, is clear that the cross was God's idea and that His holiness, His will, is revealed in it.

> To wit, that God was in Christ, reconciling the world unto himself, not imputing their trespasses unto them; and hath committed unto us the word of reconciliation.
>
> —2 Corinthians 5:19

> Herein is love, not that we loved God, but that he loved us, and sent his Son to be the propitiation for our sins.
>
> —1 John 4:10

> For God so loved the world, that he gave his only begotten Son, that whosoever believeth in him should not perish, but have everlasting life. For God sent not his Son into the world to condemn the world; but that the world through him might be saved.
>
> —John 3:16–17

Holiness

Our hope of salvation is not a love-hate rupture in the Godhead, with one third saving humanity from another much angrier third while another third floats around the room. Our great hope, our *only* hope, is the holiness of God. On the cross, Jesus was not saving us from the holiness of God. He was proving it! The cross is a window on the soul of God. Jesus is called the "Lamb slain from the foundation of the world" (Rev. 13:8). In the sacrifice on Calvary, I AM died for humanity. God is perfect personhood. He cannot be less than perfect in all three persons. I AM is always I AM. In all three persons He is true to His own unchanging, unchangeable, ultimate, perfect holiness.

In other churches the sacrificial purpose of the cross is itself sacrificed in favor of a solitary Father, loving, universally saving, and apparently embarrassed by all that bloody, unfortunate business on Calvary. In still others, the Holy Spirit has evidently worked a *coup d'état*, taking over heaven's radio station and declaring Himself in charge.

I once preached in a large independent church in Australia, after which the pastor explained why I would not be invited back. "You are preaching the Spirit of Jesus. We used to preach that, but now we believe in the Holy Spirit. We have moved on, and your message doesn't fit here anymore."

I was shocked, of course, to discover that the Spirit of Jesus and the Holy Spirit had gone through a divorce and I had not heard of it. I decided to pursue the matter even though I sensed intuitively that I was not going to like the answer.

"I know it's just crazy old me, but I would have said that the Spirit of Jesus and the Holy Spirit were the same."

"Oh, no," he explained. "The Spirit of Jesus teaches people how to give away their car. That's what you preach. The Holy Spirit teaches people how to get a better one. That's what we preach."

I was so glad he cleared that up. When the holiness of God, the perfect personhood of divine character, is fractured, pygmy theologians set one person of the Trinity against another and drift into idiotic heresies that hurt people and don't even make sense.

If God is always the same, one question must be answered immediately. What is God, in all three persons, always like? The answer afforded

21

by 1 John 4:8 is marvelous indeed and magnificent in its simplicity. "God is love."

That simple statement is in itself a three-in-one. The whole and its three parts are proper entities. I AM is holiness. Holiness is love. God is love!

"I'm no theologian," a certain radio preacher once began. "I'm just a country preacher."

In the light of the confused sermon that followed, one was forced to agree. Every believer, lay or ordained, *must* be a theologian. Theology is quite simply what one believes to be true about God. It is my experience that those who claim not to be theologians are usually just bad ones.

If a woman sees God as an angry, demanding, impossible-to-please stepfather-in-the-sky, her "Christianity" will reflect a bound-up, neurotic perfectionism. Likewise, the God of the nominal church-goer is the distant, insensitive, absentee landlord to whom homage must be paid twice a year. His is a "nursing-home-God," a doddering, yet respected, senile old uncle who demands little, offers less, and is satisfied with a check and an occasional visit.

The God of holiness so far transcends such

pitiful concepts as to make them laughable if they were not so sad. To simply say "God is love" is quite insufficient unless that affirmation is received personally in the light of a biblical concept of God. "God is love" must be understood to mean God is love in *my* life. "God is love" must become "God loves *me*." I know that God loves me because He acts, wills, and emotes consistently with His own nature. His will for *me* must be good because He is good. His Word must be true in *my* life because He is Truth. He must love *me* because He is Love.

One contemporary speaker said that there is "something about me that turns God on." That is tenuous ground for any relationship. What if that which is fetching to God today were gone tomorrow? I need to know there is an unchangeableness to God's love because I, unfortunately, am constantly changing.

What if God loves me because I am kind and gentle? That is all well and good until I shout at my kids on the way to Sunday school. The God who was "turned on" by my sweet disposition is now put off by my ugly impatience. That means that today God loves me because I have been good, looked good, served well, preached with an anointing, prayed properly, or washed the car. If God is as fickle as I am, His emotions as undependable as ours, and His love no more sure, what hope have we in His nature?

There is nothing I can do to make God love me more. I cannot pray enough, get sanctified enough, win enough people to Jesus, or be clever enough to make God love me more. How can I hope by my actions to make perfect love more perfect?

By the same token I cannot make God love me any less. I cannot sin enough, hate enough, or even deny God enough to make Perfect Love, love me less!

If God is I AM, and if I AM is perfect love, then God is perfect love to *me*. That is the key. We must see that God's love *me-ward* is magnificently *personal*. God's holiness is not just a force field of sterile, laboratory morality somewhere over the rainbow. Perfect love is I AM to *me*. I am never in the corner of His affections. I am never forgotten, never in the suburbs of His love, and He is never, ever too busy for me. I am His only project. I am in the center of His heart and the apple of His eye. All of the creative faculties that spoke light into existence

24

are fixed, without distraction.

The miracle of God's love is decidedly *not* that there is enough for the whole human race. That "crumbs under the table" theology says that God's love is so huge that every man everywhere can get a little. That little crumb, of course, being so wonderful is quite sufficient. No, no, *no!* That makes God sound like an old woman at a USO club trying to stretch the last of the *agape* mayonnaise to make sandwiches for all the hungry soldiers.

The miracle of God's love is not that there is enough for all to receive a crumb. The miracle is that we each receive it all. That is *omnipresence*. That God is everywhere does not mean a little of Him is in all places, but that *all* of Him is everywhere. So it is with His love. It is not so much that God has enough love to go around. It is rather that I am the sole object of the affections of Jehovah God. God does not merely have enough love for all of us. He loves each of us with all He is, because He can never be a partial God to anyone. He is, in other words, holy.

If we could only understand this one truth, how it would set us free. We would never again labor to earn the love of God. We would never again experience depression or fear that our sins have changed God. How liberated is the believer whose God never changes!

Some years ago at a small holiness college in the Midwest, the gruesomely mutilated body of a student was found in his room. The county coroner sealed off the blood-drenched dormitory room as a crime scene. To her it appeared an obvious and brutal homicide, but the local pastor quietly yet steadfastly maintained it was a suicide.

"Suicide?" the coroner demanded. "How can a boy inflict dozens of savage wounds on himself? He would have passed out. College kids who commit suicide take poison. They don't slaughter themselves with butcher knives."

She was wrong. The forensic investigation proved conclusively that it was indeed a suicide! After the inquest the coroner visited the pastor at his home. "You knew this was a suicide. How could a boy do that?"

The pastor explained that if a person's obsessive drive for perfection is met by enough failure, self-hatred and lethal self-loathing can be the result. The boy was killing his worst enemy because he could not measure up to some false standard of holiness.

What had the boy done? Who knows! Maybe an impure thought had lodged in his brain. Perhaps some immature habit continued to dog him. Perhaps it was outright sin. The answer is hardly important. What is important is that a college boy is dead, and his family grieves in confusion.

Meanwhile, just a few states away, a multimillion-dollar ministry empire crumbled around the slumped shoulders of its fallen hero. The Christian community watched in horrified dismay as the whole grimy story unfolded like a seamy novel. Sexual indecency and extravagance made a laughingstock of Christianity.

A mature woman lives in spiritual frustration for decades, a guilt-ridden college boy takes his own life, and a glitzy preacher falls into materialism and gross immorality. What can these desperate tragedies possibly have in common?

The tragic common denominator in all three is that each failed to understand the holiness of God. In God's holiness we find neither hopelessness nor blasé permission. His holiness is not the impenetrable barrier that keeps me away. Holiness is the love that ripped open the veil.

Holiness

The holiness of God, unchanged by the post-modern climate of constantly mutating values and truths, remains the great cosmic constant. Unceasing, unchanging, and unalloyed, the holiness of Father, Son, and Spirit is not just hopeful. It is our only hope.

Chapter 6

Inside Out

TWO YANKEES from Minnesota, traveling through South Georgia, knocked the muffler off their car. Pulling into a local junkyard in search of a replacement, the two men met the owner, a good ol' boy in coveralls and lace-up brogans. He explained the situation to them in a deep drawl.

"Ya'll can go in and find one if you want. It's near closing time, and I don't have the time to look. If you find what you want, you can have it. But I better warn you that in my junkyard there are two problems. One is the bottomless pit. Fall in it, and you'll never be seen again. The other is my Rottweiler. He will kill you if he can."

Desperate for the muffler, the men from Minnesota cautiously made their way into the junkyard. Sure enough, they soon found themselves at the edge of a hole with no apparent bottom. Resting on its very lip was an old, burned-out engine block. Desiring to see how deep the hole was, the two rolled the engine block in. Surely they could hear such a heavy thing hit the bottom, no matter how deep it was.

As they waited for the engine block to hit bottom, the feared Rottweiler suddenly appeared behind them. Fangs bared, foaming at the mouth, and snarling like a wolf, the beast hurtled through the air straight at them. Before they could react, the demonic beast shot past them and disappeared into the hole.

Shaken, the two northerners decided to forget the muffler. At the gate was the smirking owner.

"Well, I see by the look on your faces you found the bottomless pit. You didn't believe me, did you?"

"Well, now we do," one of the Minnesotans answered. "We found the pit. But I'm afraid we have some bad news for you. Your Rottweiler just ran and jumped down in that hole and disappeared. I believe your dog has leapt to his death."

"That just don't seem likely," the junk dealer explained. "I had him chained to an old engine block."

We chain our souls to how we think about God and His holiness. Fix your eternity to a concept that plunges into the pit, and you are going in with it. Fasten your eternity to unchanging truth, and it will take you heavenward.

God is always I AM, always who He is. Still the question remains, is He a moral God? In other words, if holiness means to be consistent in nature, could a holy God be consistently bad? It may seem like a silly question to many, but, in fact, the question would make a great deal of sense to some non-Christians.

Consider these two philosophical propositions:

- Proposition I: God is holy because He does not sin.
- Proposition II: God does not sin because He is holy.

Both contain not only the same number of words, but exactly the same eight words, only slightly rearranged. Can such a minor reordering really change the meaning all that much? Into the narrow gap between these two statements, all human hope, like the hapless Rottweiler, can plunge into the bottomless pit.

If Proposition I is true, we envision God striving to follow the rules in *THE GOD MANUAL*. We optimistically reckon that He can do it. He is, after all, God. The problem is that if we define God as holy by His actions, we define in the horrifying possibility that His actions might change. As long as God does good, He is holy; therefore, if He ever does evil, He is not holy. If that should happen, the universe and our peace plummet into a black hole of terrifying possibilities. Consider an all-powerful God free to do evil at His whim. That is simply too mind-bogglingly horrible to contemplate.

On the other hand, if Proposition II is true, God's actions are the result, not the determinant, of His character. God is not what He does. God does who He is. Scripture is clear that love, for example, is not one of the nifty things God does, but it is the essence of who I AM is. His will for my life is not good because He decides in my particular case for it to be good. The will of God is good, has to be good, must be good, because I AM is good.

In the trying seasons of life, this truth gives great hope. We are never in a tough spot because God got in a snit. Even in my darkest valley, even in chastisement, I know His will for me is good because of the holiness of God.

Fastening theology to a limited or wrong

view of God's holiness plays havoc with faith in every way. Prayer, for example, is crippled by error. Many, not only in the world but also in the church, are timid in prayer because of a misbegotten concept of God as the Cosmic Receptionist. God, the harried "answerer of all the incoming calls," labors night and day to respond. He can do it most of the time because He is God and because at any given moment, at least half the world is asleep. I even heard one pastor, a pastor mind you, say that he liked to pray at 3 a.m. because he had God's full attention. If he was joking, it wasn't funny. If he was not joking, he actually put into words what many subconsciously believe. Evidently if you pray in an hour of peak calls, you may get a recording or a busy signal, or be put on hold, waiting with a deep need while listening to some recording of angelic elevator music.

It is God's holiness, His completeness meward in perfect love, that makes me know that I am God's only concern. I never have the partial attention of a distracted God, hurrying me out of His office so that He can deal with the next case. I am I AM's only concern, all He thinks of, all He cares about. All His creative power, all His love, and all His grace are mine. The miracle of omnipresence is not that part of a gaseous god is everywhere at once. That is *not* holiness. The glorious truth is that *all* of God is everywhere, all at once. I am God's only project. So is everyone else, all at the same time. That is the joy of the holiness of God.

An elderly woman in a certain church wept uncontrollably when she realized the very holiness of God that she feared and nearly hated was in fact the assurance that God loved her.

"O God," she sobbed in my arms. "My whole life I ached to make God love me. Just for one day I wanted to feel absolutely acceptable to God. But every time I felt envy or got too tired to go to church on Wednesday night, I knew I couldn't quite measure up."

Dear God, forgive us! How many sweet old ladies who have cut their teeth on holiness teaching have broken their own hearts trying to please a God they never really knew? What a tragedy!

I remember laughing in spite of myself at a comedian-impressionist being questioned on the BBC. The comedian was brilliant. His hilarious answers were given through impressions of celebrities. I marveled that he could so easily change from Oprah Winfrey to Larry King to George W. Bush. One exchange, however, deeply touched my heart.

"Don't you ever get afraid," the interviewer asked, "that you will get stuck in one character or another?"

The studio audience and I obliged the newscaster with a laugh at the odd question, but when the camera zoomed in for a close-up on the face of the comedian, he was visibly moved. The question had struck home, and his countenance sobered.

"My darkest fear," he somberly answered, "is that I will wake up one morning and be able to do Harrison Ford and Madonna, but I won't remember how to do *me* anymore."

That is not merely his own personal fear, but it is the corporate nightmare of twenty-first-century humanity. We postmoderns live such fractured lives that we are in danger of losing track of ourselves. We are one person at the office, another with friends, another with spouse and kids, and still another at church or all alone. Are there enough pieces of us to be lover, boss, employee, customer, stepchild, doctor, priest, or lawyer?

Holiness

The wail of the postmodern is the cry of the Gadarene demoniac: "My name is Legion." With life splintered like a broken mirror, we search desperately for wholeness in diversion, dissipation, and discipline. Confronted again and again by our own multiple images, we find nothing but distortion and brokenness. Each finger of the shattered mirror may give a "true" reflection in some part. The parts, held together by a "frame" of sorts, may even remain contiguous, but the jagged reality is a shattered, pitiful reflection of wholeness longed for and lost.

A spate of high-profile corporate and political scandals, an agonizing drip, drip, drip of scandal, has left America shell-shocked about leadership. What is happening on Wall Street is but the tip of a moral iceberg threatening to sink the Titanic of western culture. It would be easier to take, perhaps, if it were not oozing in over the threshold of the church.

The president of a large ministry told me that a long-time friend and prayer partner so egregiously cheated his ministry in a business deal that a protracted and bitter lawsuit resulted. When his friend was convicted of several crimes in another matter, the man claimed that he was being persecuted for his faith. It was a shattering private disillusionment for that ministry leader, very like the numbing effect of public scandals on postmodern America.

A wave of public leadership disconnected from private wickedness is making us a cynical nation, people content with broken, shattered lives. Furthermore, we expect no better from our leaders. This new generation, reeling from blow after blow, medicating itself with comedians and cocaine, does not hate the church or the gospel. They just want to see the real thing. Disgusted with the jaded detachment of their parents, the millennial generation is looking for hope, and the hope they need is holiness—true holiness.

Some who readily agree that God is holy deny the possibility of holiness in the life of the believer. God is holy, they reason, because God is God, but we are mortal and, therefore, incapable of holiness. That is not what God thinks.

> Ye shall be holy: for I the LORD your God
> am holy.
>
> —LEVITICUS 19:2

A student of mine asked if that statement was a command or a promise. The answer is *yes*. It

Holiness

is a command, to be sure. God wants holy children, wholly dedicated, wholly consecrated and wholly His. He wants children who have holy hearts and who live holy lives. He commands us to be children like that. Still we know God will not expect of us that which we cannot do. He provides that which He commands.

The question that follows is obvious: what is true holiness?

The holiness and Pentecostal movement of the early and mid-twentieth century was certain of the answer. Don't go to movies; don't wear makeup or short dresses; now you're holy. Simple, and simply wrong. Beyond being wrong, it was destructive, producing a second and third generation of Pentecostal and holiness Christians that were wounded and angry reactionaries, impossible to lead and cantankerous to pastor.

The real problem arises, however, when a sweet little granny who has attended three holiness camp meetings a year for sixty years tells herself she is holy because she wears no lipstick. Yet when a lovely teenage girl wearing lipstick sits near her in church, she hates that girl for having the audacity to be young, pretty, and happy! This inconsistency between internal reality and outward appearance is stuccoed tidily each year at camp meeting until it is no longer noticed. Hurt, frustrated, and unloving, she is an outward model of "holiness," yet she lives a joyless life in a straitjacket—the rules—while growing annually more brittle and barren.

When the heart of holiness is embittered by life, it is because its theology is pickled in law. John Wesley said, "Sour godliness is the devil's religion." A tragic flaw of the holiness movement has been its inability to speak meaningfully to the modern suburbanite living in a madhouse of sin. The holiness movement will continue to fail evangelistically until it enriches its vocabulary to include a few more words than *no* and *don't*. The holiness movement is in danger of studying Wesleyan theology while Rome burns around its ears.

The last quarter of the twentieth century saw the meteoric rise of the Charismatic movement, which rediscovered "where the Spirit of the Lord is, there is liberty" (2 Cor. 3:17). Casting aside the laws of the past two generations, the Charismatics began exploring the frontiers of that scripture with a vengeance. By the close of the century, the Charismatic movement had produced and destroyed huge ministries that sprang up like mushrooms and withered in a night. Sexual scandals, financial mismanagement, and flamboyant lifestyles quickly overwhelmed the innocent, abandoned joy of its initial phase. Broken churches and broken lives lay in the wake of the Charismatic movement just as anger and frustration had followed the holiness movement.

The holiness and traditional Pentecostal crowd abused holiness and the Charismatics bypassed it, and both are now gasping for breath. Badly needed now is a fresh articulation of holiness, without which no man shall see the Lord. (See Hebrews 12:14.)

God, whose actions flow from His will, promises His children holiness like His own. The Pharisees could not wash their hands often enough or right enough to cleanse their hearts. Holiness from the outside in did not work for them, or for the holiness camp meeting folks, or the classical Pentecostals, or anyone else. It never works.

What works—and it does work—is holiness from the inside out. Many years ago the preschool daughter of a close friend brought a mangled rosebud to her parents as they and my wife and I were drinking coffee on their porch. Her question was that of a child.

"Daddy, how come when God opens a flower, it's so pretty, and when I do it, it looks like this?"

Then, quickly, as only a child can do, she answered her own question. "Oh, I know! It's because God does it from the inside."

From out of the burning bush God spoke to Moses first of His own holiness. Then He spoke of holiness of heart in the sinful humanity to whom He sent Moses as deliverer.

"Moses, put your hand into your shirt, and then pull it out again."

When Moses obeyed, his hand was covered in leprosy. That must have been a thrilling miracle moment for Moses. I suspect Moses was thinking, *Hey, this is great, Lord. You call me at eighty to return to Egypt where there is a price on my head. You tell me to lead a nation of stiff-necked slaves into the wilderness, and finally, you give me leprosy. This is a wonderful day in the neighborhood.*

"Now," God told Moses, "do it again. Put your hand in your shirt one more time, and then look at it."

This time Moses' hand was completely healed. (See Exodus 4:6–7.) Among all that God was saying in that incident, He must surely have been making the connection between heart and hand. What I do with my hands will never for very long out-distance the condition of my heart.

The hidden leprosy of inward sin will doggedly resist the exorcism of outward observance. Sooner or later sin will surface, even erupt into action. One cannot stay away from bad movies long enough to create a changed heart. A pure heart, however, will, sooner or later, change the movies I want to see. My friend's daughter was right. God does it from the inside.

The school or church that enforces a strict dress code is invariably accused of being legalistic. They may be. However, they may not be. They may simply be strict, which is *not* the same thing as legalism. The legalist views the entire universe as an if-then philosophical proposition. "If I raise my kids right, then…" "If I pray correctly and have enough faith, then…" Always, if something, then something.

One may be a legalist in more than one area of life. The confessional faith legalist, the true purist in the field, is confident that if he, or anyone, will confess his faith correctly and pray with proper faith, then he will have that for which he prays. He refuses to be confused with such minor issues as the sovereignty of God. If …then, says the faith legalist.

Unlike the so-called "faith" crowd in many ways, the legalist in the parenting realm may mock the legalism of "confess it and posses it," and then act the same way in his parenting. In fact, one famous family teacher said, "You show me what is wrong with your child, and I'll tell you what you did wrong as a parent."

A more legalistic and wickedly destructive statement can hardly be imagined. Here's my question. If the son of a sinless father still sins, is that father to blame for his son's sins? If so, God is to blame for Adam, and that is blasphemy. Adam sinned. Tell me what God did wrong.

The lie of legalism is that every spiritual reality can be explained by either breaking or keeping a law. Holiness legalists want to find a cause-and-effect relationship between what people do and the condition of their hearts. In fact, no such law exists. The heart dictates action, not vice versa, and a clean heart is a work of grace.

In mathematics an integer is defined as any positive or negative whole number. Eight is an integer. Eight and one-half is not. Wholeness is at the heart of the definition of an integer. There is another English word that relates to this mathematical idea: *integrity*. God is holy because he is the Ultimate Integer. He is perfect integrity, divine wholeness, and fractionless personhood. It is wholeness that God commands, and wholeness that He promises.

Poor Humpty Dumpty, broken into a thousand pieces, could not be restored by his own efforts or by all the king's horses and men. Only the King Himself could do it. It is God's pleasure to bring wholeness to the shattered and restore integrity to fractional lives. Only a fresh outpouring of the Spirit of holiness can produce holy living by men made whole. From Ephesus to Aldersgate Street, in every great move of the Holy Spirit, whole people, sanctified people, people of integrity surfaced to change history and civilization.

The great work of the Holy Spirit is not to cookie-cut little gingerbread Christians. Nor is it to pound rebellious teenage boys into shorter haircuts. His work is to make broken lives whole. Romans 1:4 states that Jesus was raised from the dead and declared to be the Son of God with power, by the Spirit of holiness. It is by that same Spirit of holiness that God raises holy people from the living death of shattered sin.

The first time the Holy Spirit is mentioned in Scripture is in Genesis 1:2: "And the earth was without form, and void; and darkness was upon the face of the deep. And the Spirit of God moved upon the face of the waters." The Wind of God brooded over the face of the abyss. Impatient and unsatisfied with chaos, He longed for God's discipline and order. God's Spirit is still striving to bring His creative character to bear on darkness and disorder. That brooding wind of God that desired to see light and life where there was darkness and chaos now hovers achingly over the life full of sin. The passion of the Spirit of God is to breathe upon humanity the very character and nature of God.

In a heart forgiven there may still linger dark, untamed passions more from the abyss than from above. Such people know they are redeemed. Their names are written in the Lamb's Book of Life. The blessed assurance of salvation is theirs by faith. Yet they find only failure at trying to walk in holiness. Newly sensitized to the convictions of the Holy Spirit, such Christians long to be obedient, loving, and holy. Year after battered year they live in fierce but frustrated determination. Anger, self-loathing, and depression are the tragic results.

Some, by temperament and constitution, are more resolute than others in resisting fleshly temptations. Yet resentments, jealousies, fears, envy, unforgiveness, and the corpus of spiritual sins that remain uncrucified belie outward holiness, revealing it to be the "will worship" that it is (Col. 2:23).

The Sirens of Greek mythology perched on the rocks around their island and sang seductively to passing ships. Their song was utterly irresistible. Knowing they would drown, knowing full well that death awaited them, sailors drove their ships on the Sirens' rocks. The mysterious pull of the Sirens' deadly song laid hold upon every sailor in every ship that passed within earshot.

Two famous captains brought their crews and ships safely past the island of the Sirens. Odysseus, knowing the danger, poured molten wax in the ears of his men and tied their hands and feet. He then strapped himself to the mast and screamed at the top of his lungs to drown the sound of the mystical singing. It was a victory of sorts, to be sure. Odysseus and his men eluded destruction, but the picture of their "safe" passage is a bound and joyless one.

Jason and his men, the fabled Argonauts, also escaped death on the rocks of the Sirens. Jason, however, hired the magic lute player, Mesmer, to travel with the Argonauts. This supernatural musician had the ability to spellbind his hearers. No listener could break free as long as he played. As soon as Jason's ship came near the island, the crew assembled on deck, and the magic lute player began to sing his captivating melodies. The Sirens, finding their own songs ignored, listened to Mesmer. At this they turned to stone, never again to lure poor sailors to death and destruction.

Some believers, like Odysseus, seem to be strapped to the mast, wax in their ears, screaming to drown the siren song of temptation. That a victory of sorts is theirs is undeniable, and when they make the harbor, safe at last, I am certain their rejoicing is great. Yet what a pathetic picture of holiness. The sons and daughters of God are not prisoners of passion, chained to the mizzen mast of dogma, longing for nothing more than heaven's eventual escape.

Raised from the dead the holy hear a heavenly rhapsody. It is a dreary holiness indeed that spends all its energy resisting sin. The joy of holiness belongs to the heart captured by a sweeter song. The joy of sanctified living has too often been forgotten as believers scurried to batten down the hatches.

It is the primary work of the Holy Ghost to so thoroughly engage the soul of a believer that the drawing power of sin is snapped. Holiness is not a burden but a delight. The sanctified saint is a dancing child, turning barefoot pirouettes on the beaches of the Red Sea and singing to the desert skies. "I will sing unto the LORD, for he hath triumphed gloriously: the horse and his rider hath he thrown into the sea" (Exodus 15:1).

The steely determination to scream right on past the island of the Sirens is admirable, of course, and certainly to be preferred over weak resignation and moral bankruptcy. In these last days, however, the Holy Spirit issues a sweeter summons: "All hands on deck to hear the lute player."

Classical holiness doctrine does not formally teach a dreary, teeth-clenching resistance to sin. The point is that in the absence of an explosive, personal experience with the Holy Spirit, mere doctrine will eventually degenerate into just such a negative approach.

When, on the other hand, I throw myself before God, broken in my brokenness, He can breathe into me the Spirit of holiness that raised Christ Jesus from the dead (Rom. 1:4). Because the Spirit of holiness is God's very wholeness, He can put Humpty Dumpty back together again. He inbreathes integrity and inspires purity, power, and love, while filtering out sin, weakness, and fear.

Chapter 4
The Finger of God

---

*E*YES ABLAZE with hellish horror, the demon-ized lad cowered in the doorway, shielding his face with his arms and whining like a trapped wolf. In a clash like cavalry at full tilt, the mighty wrestling match was underway. The boy's pitiable shrieks and guttural howls were terrible to hear. Jesus of Nazareth was contesting for the spirit, mind, and body of an unnamed mute held in bondage by the forces of evil. In the end the lad was free, delivered from demons and ready for a new life.

In the context of this great act of healing (Luke 11) Jesus gave us perhaps the greatest of all teachings on the Spirit of holiness. The setting was appropriate because the Spirit of God's power is less suitable for analysis in a vacuum than in a demonstration of power. The storm of controversy that raged around Jesus reached hurricane force on that day. Pharisees and scribes, perfectly willing for the poor, mute wretch to go on in demonized bondage, were outraged when Jesus set him free. Their anger was more than predictable.

It was when His word was manifested in power that Jesus signed His own death warrant. When His sermons on the kingdom of God found expression in a ministry of power so obviously lacking among the Pharisees, their fury was predictable and deadly.

> But some of them said, He casteth out devils through Beelzebub the chief of the devils.
>
> —LUKE 11:15

Jesus demolished that specious logic with one sentence: "Every kingdom divided against itself is brought to desolation; and a house divided against a house falleth" (v. 17). In other words, Jesus demanded, "Is Satan possessing such people as this and then casting himself out?" The answer was absurdly obvious, and the Pharisees fell silent. Then even as He foiled their blasphemous defamation with one rhetorical question, He devastated their pride with a second.

> And if I by Beelzebub cast out devils, by whom do your sons cast them out?
>
> —LUKE 11:19

51

That is to say, "By one power or another, this boy's demons are out. The lad is free! He can speak! By what power do your sons, your ilk, your kind—by what power do you and yours cast out demons?"

The inescapable answer was that they could not cast them out at all. The penury of their ministry was brought under terrible indictment by the power of Christ's words. Now the hellish hornet's nest of envy was shown for what it was—demonic, self-centered religiosity. Having neither holiness nor power in supernatural ministry, the Pharisees were perfectly willing to libel Christ.

Having dismissed them with a simple argument, Jesus gave us a foundational teaching on kingdom living in the power of the Holy Spirit. This rich blend of word and deed includes not only the exchange with the Pharisees but also the "Lord's Prayer" and the glorious promise of Luke 11:13. The passage is a declaration of God's plan and intention of restoration, and a call to full devotion. The first twenty-three verses of Luke 11 are perhaps the most arresting and challenging body of teaching on the Holy Spirit and the kingdom of God in the New Testament.

Having summarily dismissed the challenge of the Pharisees, Jesus boldly declared, "But if I with the *finger of God* cast out devils, no doubt the kingdom of God is come upon you" (v. 20, emphasis added). The *finger of God* is a Hebrew idiom for the Holy Spirit. In fact, the account in the Gospel of Matthew uses the phrase "the Holy Spirit" (Matt. 12:28). Jesus' statement reveals that supernatural ministry in the power of the Spirit is a sign of the kingdom of God.

When Adam surrendered to pride and sin, he also yielded to Satan the authority and dominion that he had been given. Satan's rejoicing was surely unmixed, for he knew that only a man, not God and not an angel, could legally reclaim that authority. The newly man-crowned "prince of the power of the air" was not about to give it back. Now, however, sin had been injected into the human race. In the face of such calamity, could God hope to raise up a "new" Adam to succeed where the first one had failed? If the first Adam had sinned in an Edenic paradise, how could his seed, surrounded by a universe in rebellion, ever hope to "bruise the serpent's head"? Satan was in the driver's seat, and he knew it.

The one utterly incalculable act of God that spelled the end of Satan's reign was the Incarnation. That in the womb of a virgin the Word of God might become human flesh, a second Adam, never dawned on the gates of hell.

Jesus said, "When a strong man armed keepeth his palace, his goods are in peace" (Luke 11:21). The "strong man" was Satan, who, armed with a demonic host and cast out of heaven in rebellion, kept his house (a fallen world) and his goods (the sons and daughters of Adam). The "someone stronger" was the Word who became flesh. Satan held humanity captive in a purse at his side until Jesus met him in the way and committed highway robbery! It was legal, however, because Jesus took back what was His to start with.

When Jesus sent out the seventy for ministry, He commanded them to heal the sick, cast out demons, and preach the gospel. What gospel? They could hardly have preached the blood of Jesus while it still flowed in His veins. The cross and the resurrection were yet to be accomplished. What, then, *did* they preach? They declared the kingdom of God, that Messiah had launched a beachhead in alien territory and the seed of woman had finally come!

By his sin, the first Adam closed the door on Eden. By His righteousness, the second Adam threw it wide open again. The first Adam brought death. The second Adam brought life. The first Adam brought the curse. The second Adam bore it away. The first Adam sealed humanity out. The second Adam welcomed humanity back in. The manifest proof that Jesus was the second Adam come to overcome the strong man was His ministry in the power of the finger of God.

An Old Testament phrase, the finger of God is absolutely fascinating. It surfaces with impact at significant moments. The finger of God actually means *the Holy Spirit*. Moses and Aaron by demonstrations of power sought to persuade Pharaoh to release the Hebrews. Pharaoh summoned his own magicians to match their power deed for deed. When Aaron's rod became a serpent, so did those of the magicians. Now certainly Aaron came out ahead in each case, but it was a "split decision." The conclusion might well have been reached that Aaron and the Egyptian magicians were both dealing in the profane powers of ancient witchcraft, until one act proved decisive. When Aaron turned dust into lice, the

Egyptian wizards were utterly defeated (Exod. 7:10–11; 8:16–18).

"Your majesty," they said in frustration, "this is the *finger of God*." That is to say, "We are not just overmatched in witchcraft. Moses and Aaron are not simply better wizards than we. They represent an entirely different kingdom, a power greater than wizardry. *This* is the *finger of God*."

In Exodus 31:18, the Law is written by the finger of God. Similarly in Zechariah 14:20, it is the finger of God that inscribes the law of separation and holiness. It is the finger of God that writes the law, and it is by the finger of God that Jesus works the works of deliverance. Can the finger of God write both liberty *and* law?

In his prophecy of the coming covenant Jeremiah shines the needed light.

> But this shall be the covenant that I will make with the house of Israel; After those days, saith the Lord, I will put my law in their inward parts, and write it in their hearts; and will be their God, and they shall be my people.
>
> —JEREMIAH 31:33

Jesus told His disciples that their holiness must exceed the holiness of the Pharisees. They could never hope to be better than the Pharisees by obeying the law. The Pharisees, after all, were quite good at it. What then could exceed the holiness of the Pharisees? Holiness of heart, wholeness of spirit, could do what the law could not.

When John proclaimed Jesus of Nazareth the "Lamb of God," he also said that Jesus was "he which baptizeth with the Holy Ghost" (John 1:33). In other words, John viewed the coming of the kingdom as the dawn of a new era. He foresaw that in the kingdom of Messiah, baptism with the Holy Spirit would be a reality.

The heart of holiness is holiness of heart. According to Jeremiah 31, the coming of Messiah would not stop the finger of God from writing the law. It would not, however, be written in tablets of stone. The New Covenant law is written in the innermost part, the heart of mankind.

The law of holiness has not been set side. We are, however, called into a new relationship with the law. To the legalist, the stone tablets of the law become a prison house. Some in the classical holiness denominations stand shoulder to the wheel, nose to the grindstone crying, "Today I shall be holy if it kills me!" It will! It surely will, and it makes the good news bad news.

Yet if we bypass holiness in the name of grace, we disregard the whole council of Scripture. Holiness is not optional equipment in the New Testament. In Romans 6:1–4, Paul speaks to this very idea.

> What shall we say then? Shall we continue in sin, that grace may abound? God forbid. How shall we that are dead to sin, live any longer therein? Know ye not, that so many of us as were baptized into Jesus Christ were baptized into his death? Therefore we are buried with him by baptism into death: that like as Christ was raised up from the dead by the glory of the Father, even so we also should walk in newness of life.

We are in danger of developing, in the name of grace, an ethical posture somewhere to the left of whoopee. Shall our liberty become license? God forbid! In every generation the finger of God does exactly what He did on Sinai's craggy brow; He writes the law of holiness. It is our relationship to that law that determines the shape of our lives. *Under* the law we become bound and brittle. *Outside* the law we become rebellious, proud, and sinful. In Jeremiah 31:33, however, we see that there remains a third possibility. No longer *under* the law that it might constrain us and never *outside* the law that it might condemn us, the law *within* will sanctify us. The great work of the Holy Spirit is to write the law. Now in the kingdom He no longer carves it in stone to stand in implacable, impersonal judgment on all men. He writes instead in the heart of mankind, HOLINESS UNTO THE LORD, and the law becomes a living fountain of sanctifying grace in man's inner being.

By seeing the Holy Spirit as the finger of God, the apparent tension between the emphases of holiness and power is fully met. He is both. It is the finger of God who writes the law of God, but it is also by, and in, the finger of God that the church's hope of a supernatural ministry is fulfilled. The Holy Spirit rested on Jesus in perfect holiness, and by it He cast out demons, healed the sick, and raised the dead.

The finger of God writes the law of holiness in the heart of the believer. This great work of heart holiness cannot be overestimated. To lose sight of it is to lose all. However, it must also be remembered that it is also by the power of the finger of God that Jesus wrought miracles, discerned spirits, and cast out devils. The union of a sanctified life and a ministry of power is holy indeed, a marriage made in heaven, a mirror of Christ, and the heartbeat of New Testament Christianity.

The question remains, "Can I, in my humanity, receive the Spirit of holiness that rested on Jesus?" Is holiness of heart a nifty theory, or can it be realized? Is holiness a personal possibility? John saw the Holy Spirit rest on Jesus Christ, but He was, after all, the Christ of God. In a deep consciousness of Christ's divinity it is easy to lose sight of His humanity. It is often forgotten that this twofold work of holiness and empowerment by the Holy Spirit is exactly what He longs to do in *all* believers. John the Baptist said that He on whom the Holy Spirit rested would also be Him who bestowed it. Certainly Jesus had no need to be cleansed from sin. Yet the point remains that the Holy Spirit came, filling and glorifying a human vessel. Holiness and power resided fully in Christ.

The Lord Himself devoted considerable time

in the passage to explaining the willingness of God to pour His Spirit into human "seekers." In a series of rather obvious parables (the midnight visitor, the hungry child, the bread, the fish, and the egg) Jesus illustrates the willingness of God to baptize humanity in the Holy Spirit.

> If ye then, being evil, know how to give good gifts unto your children: how much more shall your heavenly Father give the Holy Spirit to them that ask him?
> —LUKE 11:13

Desperate for employment, a depression-era farmer applied at a passing circus. At the circus office door he made an impassioned plea. "I'll do anything."

At this the manager's eyes lit up. "You're hired," he fairly shouted, embracing the shocked farmer. "I need a new gorilla. The old one has died, and we cannot afford to import one. We have skinned old Kong out, and I need someone to wear the suit and do the gorilla act."

All reluctance dissolved at the mention of a sizable salary. Pride gave way to necessity, and the farmer's new career was launched. As it turned out, the wheat farmer turned ape-man rather enjoyed it. His act was dramatic and crowd pleasing. He would swing out over the lion's cage on a rope and rain bananas on the enraged beast below. The rope was carefully measured, however, and any actual danger seemed minimal.

At a kiddie matinee in Oklahoma, a miscalculation brought catastrophe, and the farmer in the gorilla suit tumbled into the lion's cage. The lion leapt upon him immediately, and placing a massive paw on the "gorilla's" shoulders, he began to roar in his face.

"Help!" the farmer screamed. "Help me! Someone please save me."

"Shut up, you fool!" the lion whispered in his ear. "You'll get us *both* fired."

Unhappily, a great deal of what passes for true Christianity is nothing more than monkey-suit religion. The calamitous condition of the contemporary church is that she has a pretty fair idea of what a Christian looks like. Granted, the view may be informed by local or cultural differences, but the fact remains that a portrait of a proper "Christian" has achieved something of a universal consensus. The primitive church at, say, Ephesus, in the first century A.D., had no such luxury. No definitions of "churchmanship," or a clear picture of Christianity in action, had come into focus. The longing for holiness among new converts quickly began to redefine cultures and reshape lives. New believers wanted to move away from Roman decadence and find higher ground, but they had little idea what a new lifestyle might look like.

The early church bloomed wildly, often without the benefit of proper clergy or church growth experts. The primitive churches sprang to life in the white heat of revival. Later, when wolves came upon them with the impossible burdens of law, the precious innocence of early faith gave way to hard rules. Despair is the poisonous by-product when revival power is replaced by legalistic holiness.

In Colossians 1:27, Paul dealt with one great fundamental issue: How do I live as a Christian? What does it even mean to live a holy life? What is the secret of true holiness?

"The secret," Paul said, "is Christ in you, the hope of glory."

On the surface it may not appear much of a secret. The implications, however, are magnificent. The secret of holiness, hidden from Moses and Abraham, and now revealed in the church, is not some move or strength to obey the law. It is not some hidden pathway of meditation or a mystical experience revealed only to a hyper-spiritual elite. The secret is simply the indwelling fullness of Christ in earthen vessels.

"Christ in you, the hope of glory."

What a glorious promise! We act differently when our hopes, longings, and aspirations reveal who is within. As Stephen fell, bloodied and broken, beneath the stones of hatred and prejudice, he spoke the words of Jesus and had the countenance of an angel. The *real* Stephen, stripped of all façade, was most clearly revealed in pain, humiliation, and death. What had been said of him, that he was full of faith and the Holy Spirit, proved true.

Many in the church know something is missing, but they do not know what to ask for. It is for their sakes, for businessmen, housewives, high school students, missionaries, and believers of every age and station who cannot seem to find the flow of real life in their faith, that baptism with the Holy Spirit must be preached. Many have believed for salvation and can articulate their assurance, but they are unable to worship, live, give, and forgive with liberty. Aware of the

Holy Spirit as comforter, guide, and companion, many have never found Him as sanctifier.

Because their good, conservative, Bible-belt understanding of what a Christian looks like is pretty clearly defined, they are able, over the years, to hide the inconsistencies and powerlessness by pulling on the same tattered old monkey suit. It is only in the crisis of the lion's cage that they are forced to face the fraudulency of their true selves.

That is why much teaching on the fruit of the Spirit falls dreadfully short. Merely documenting what the fruit is, while leaving its production to the hearers, only leads disciples into deeper despair because, try as they might, they are never able to manufacture the fruit. An apple is an apple because it is the product of an apple tree. It has about it the nature of "apple-ness." The Christian life filled with the Spirit of Jesus will bear His nature in the very same way. The fruit, the manner of speech, the character, attitudes, and longings of a life reveal the nature of the tree. "Godliness" like "apple-ness" is the manifest witness of the spirit of the tree. The fruit of the Spirit in Galatians 5 is a composite moral portrait of Jesus. It is futile to attempt to manufacture such divine fruit in one's own power. Apart from a true work of the Spirit of Jesus, the flesh is just tying wax apples on barren branches. The only hope for holiness is "Christ in me, the hope of glory," Christ's joy, Christ's love, and Christ's power in ministry.

Many years ago a medical missionary in West Africa was visited by an inquisitive bishop. The bishop toured the hospital, met the patients, saw the many churches that had been built, and sensed the general spirit of revival. "Tell me," the bishop said, "about your first convert here. How long were you here before your first conversion?"

"Four years, Bishop. When we first came to this country, the people utterly rejected my gospel. They would not even hear it. They came to the clinic and accepted my medicine. Yet no matter what I did, they wouldn't even come in the chapel or listen to me preach. Our first child was born shortly after we arrived, a sweet little fellow that I loved more than life itself. When he was four years old, he contracted a jungle fever and died. It hit me like a hammer blow. I dug his tiny grave in a clearing and buried him with my own hands. Then I fell on my knees and

sobbed. Four years of frustration, hurt, and disillusionment flowed out of me in a river of tears.
I looked up and saw the village chief watching
me. I had been declaring the victory of Christ
for four years, now I was blubbering like a baby
at our first real crisis. That only made me weep
more!

"Suddenly the chief ran into the village, and
he assembled all the people. He told me that
now they would hear my message. I preached by
my son's little grave, and many were saved that
day. What that chief told the village changed our
ministry."

"What did he say to the village?" the aston-
ished bishop asked.

"He weeps!" the missionary said. "The chief
told them, 'Come quickly; the missionary is
weeping. He is a real man.'"

"You see, Bishop," the missionary continued,
"I arrived here with my white skin and pale eyes,
and they thought I wasn't altogether human. In
death and pain they saw my humanity unmasked,
and they came into the kingdom."

"But wait," the flustered bishop protested.
"That is against everything I believe about the
goodness of God. Are you telling me that your

little son had to die so that they could come into the kingdom?"

"I am only a doctor," the missionary replied. "You are the theologian. But it seems to me that is what God did with His Son."

That is *exactly* what God did! "Though he were a Son, yet learned he obedience by the things which he suffered" (Heb. 5:8). In the agony of the cross Christ proved forever the reality of His humanity. In His life and ministry He proved both the power and the holiness of the Spirit in an earthen vessel.

God is willing to baptize believers with the Holy Spirit. Jesus told us to ask. Why then are we not filled? Since God is not the variable, the answer must lie either in the seeker or in the seeking, or both.

The true Pentecostal blessing will not be found by glib experience-mongers hoping for a high voltage tingle. Baptism in the Spirit is the fruit of full surrender, not the coincidental by-product of being "slain in the Spirit." It is no accident that both the record of Christ's ministry of deliverance in Luke 11 and His teaching on the Holy Spirit were prefaced by the Lord's Prayer. In the promise of Luke 11:13, the condition of verse 2 is easily overlooked. "Thy kingdom come. Thy will be done, as in heaven, so in earth" (Luke 11:2). The Master proved that He was the master teacher by the progression He developed in Luke 11:1–23.

The will of God...the kingdom of God...the Spirit of God...the finger of God...

There is no small body of literature on the kingdom of God, usually written with particular emphasis on rights, privileges, and blessings. References to prosperity and general blessedness have reached the saturation point in much contemporary Christian writing and music. Certainly the blessedness of the children of the King is not even arguable. Who would *want* to argue it? However, there is one funny thing about kingdoms. A kingdom is not a kingdom without a king. In our mad dash to the blessing bar, the church must remember exactly who is Lord. The key that unlocks the power of the kingdom is the kingship of Christ. "Thy kingdom come. Thy will be done in earth, as it is in heaven" (Matt. 6:10).

Whenever our will is done, we live in our kingdom. When His will is done, we live in His. The prayer that gains the full blessing of Pentecost is the prayer of full surrender to the lordship of Jesus Christ. We do not have to "talk God out of" Spirit baptism. He longs to pour His Holy Spirit into ready vessels. However, He absolutely will *not* fill a vessel He does not own. When we declare our Savior to be our King, we begin to live in His kingdom. We can be baptized in the Spirit of His own holiness. He comes in wind and fire to cleanse *and* to empower us.

It is not necessary that we choose between an emphasis on personal holiness and an empowered, gifted ministry. In fact, we do so at our own peril. The finger of God is the Spirit of power, the fire of sanctifying grace, and the only hope of holiness for a wounded and sin-sick world. Having committed adultery with Bathsheba and conspiring to have her husband killed, King David somehow found his way back to God. His repentance is memorialized forever by his own hand in Psalm 51. With heartrending eloquence David pleads for forgiveness and believes. His Old Testament faith in the cleansing power of the blood is stirring, his imagery magnificent, and his brokenness complete. The poignant language of Psalm 51 beautifully expresses the true contrition of a broken sinner.

Then David reaches past a humble plea for

forgiveness, far beyond it in fact, to a whole new petition. His faith for forgiveness resting in the blood, the poet-king pleads for more—sanctification.

> Create in me a clean heart, O God; and renew a right spirit within me.
>
> —PSALM 51:10

That is the holiness prayer in its essence. Not just forgiven but freed, not just cleansed of the past but liberated for the future—that is David's prayer. It is also a proper prayer for every believer.

> *Come, Spirit of holiness that raised Christ from the dead. Raise me as well to holiness of heart and life. Sanctify me wholly, and set me free to serve you in joy. Breathe, O breathe, Thy loving Spirit into my troubled breast. Let me now in Thee inherit, let me find that sacred rest.*

Pray it in faith. Now believe, breathe, and receive. Now praise Him! Rejoice in the God of holiness who imparts His nature to them that believe.

Chapter 5

Shards on the Altar

An EXPENSIVE New York jewelry store displayed a fabulous collection of ornate crosses for sale. They were incredibly beautiful and exorbitantly priced. Underneath, however, was this intriguing sign: *"These Crosses on Easy Terms."*

The cross of Christ never comes on easy terms. The key to Pentecostal power is brokenness. Holy Spirit baptism is not for those who want stylish crosses on easy terms. The key to life in the supernatural power of God is death to the grasp of the world. The corrupting clutch of worldliness will not be shaken off easily. It is a fight to the death, for sin holds us in our own grasp. The irony of sin is that Satan's only real hope to control my life is *me*. We often labor under the misguided notion that Satan wants us to do *his* will. Satan has no will in our lives. He only wants us to do *our* will. We have met the enemy, and he is us.

I once read an anthropological study of an

ancient temple in India. Its altar area was literally buried under a mountain of broken pottery. The people in that region were expert pottery makers who regularly sacrificed the fruit of their craft to their god. Having created a masterpiece, a work that stood to gain him the most fame and profit, a craftsman would take it into the temple and smash it to pieces before his stone god. The broken fragments meant that in sacrificial worship that craftsman had given up all hope of gain from the vessel. In one shattering moment the dedicated vessel was surrendered, impossible to be reclaimed. That is a perfect picture of what Hudson Taylor called "the exchanged life." Only when I am a broken vessel on the altar of a living God can I know the power of his life in and through me.

David Seamands once said, "We receive the Holy Spirit broken in our brokenness." Brokenness is our lot by virtue of Adam's fall and by our own wretched sin. As long as we cling to our brokenness, owning it to ourselves, trying to impose on it some fleshly semblance of wholeness, we will never know God's power. When the pride of self-ownership is broken by our brokenness and we see ourselves as we really are, we cast the shards of our lives at His feet, and He alone restores them to wholeness. Those who offer Him silver and gold shall be had in derision. A broken heart He gladly accepts. The King of Glory condescends to bestow His wholeness upon ruined, broken pieces the moment they rest on the altar. Whatever touches the altar is sanctified by the altar.

There are two sides to sanctification. There is that sense in which *I* sanctify myself to God. At the same time *my* dedication must be fully met by His work of grace. *He* must sanctify *me* to Himself. The miracle is not that sinners surrender their broken lives on His altar. The true miracle is that He receives those lives and declares them acceptable in His sight.

The verses at the end of Zechariah are provocative indeed.

> In that day shall there be upon the bells of the horses, HOLINESS UNTO THE LORD; and the pots in the LORD's house shall be like the bowls before the altar. Yea, every pot in Jerusalem and in Judah shall be holiness unto the LORD of hosts.
> —ZECHARIAH 14:20–21

To the ancient Jew these must have been strange words indeed. Everyone knew the sacred bowls and vessels dedicated for use only in the Lord's house were not the same as a common saucepan in a squalid hut. Yet the prophet said both must be holy. Holiness is not just for the "religious" parts of my life. Peeling potatoes, no less than prayer, belongs to God. Saturday night, no less than Sunday morning, must bear the sacred inscription: "Holiness unto the Lord." Zechariah says that even the tiniest, ornamental bridle bells must be consecrated to God as the altar vessels. The most peripheral, "unreligious" aspect of life must be as dedicated as a prayer meeting.

The frivolity of some leaders with respect to worldliness and sensuality is an embarrassment to the whole body of Christ. Too much has been excused in the name of the liberty of the Spirit. It is past time that we lovingly confront some really glaring inconsistencies in the body of Christ. Surely there is some way we can point out that Spirit-filled women really ought not to look like streetwalkers. Spirit-filled businessmen and attorneys cannot continue in the cutthroat ethics of the world. We cannot sanctify our hearts by changing our wardrobes or habits, but surely, *surely,* inner holiness will eventually reach our wardrobes and habits.

Holiness talk is not the same as sanctification. Some of the most cold-blooded, cold-eyed, gossipy, backbiting, unloving, waspish, uncharitable people in the church are virtual holiness hounds. Some who would never touch a cigarette politic in church fights with ruthless fury.

Neither loveless doctrine nor flippant disregard for holy living will touch the postmodern world. The message this generation needs is nothing more or less than scriptural Christianity. It is the message of the changed heart, baptized in love, separated unto God and ministering in apostolic power! The church, the sanctified holy church with all its graces and all its gifts intact, is the only instrument of sufficient power to address this poor confused generation.

Among the onlookers at Pentecost were a few of those particularly doubtful skeptics who dismissed the upper room fireworks as common drunkenness. Simon Peter refuted this claim with a brilliant stroke of simple logic. He pointed out the improbability of getting 120 men and women falling down, babbling drunk before nine o'clock in the morning.

In a way, however, those in the upper room were "under the influence." Filled with the Holy Spirit, they were swept up in a power beyond themselves and beyond anything they had ever known. They had imbibed the new wine of the kingdom.

Paul embroidered on this same theme in Ephesians 5:18 when he said, "And be not drunk with wine, wherein is excess; but be filled with the Spirit."

Paul's use of the metaphor is intriguing. As the alcohol content in the blood rises, it alters the personality. A person may feel a temporary wave of happiness as it is absorbed through the capillaries. Often there is a heightened sense of well-being and confidence as the warm glow of alcoholic euphoria blurs the definitions of reality.

The Holy Spirit works like that, only in reverse. As the Spirit of holiness begins to penetrate the mind, spirit, and body, reality is brought into its proper eternal perspective. As the warping of sin that twists and distorts life is suddenly struck away, the soul finds joy in its newfound liberty. Inebriated on truth, the unfettered soul delights in a liberated celebration of gifts and graces long buried under the burdens and the bondage.

Is it any wonder that observers at Pentecost ascribed the exuberance of the believers to drunkenness? They *were* drunk! The Spirit of perfect love had suddenly banished their fear. Blurred lives were suddenly brought into focus. Without warning, grieving spirits burst into flame with joy unspeakable.

My sweetest recollection of the days immediately following my own experience of the baptism in the Holy Spirit is of an early morning stroll. I recall how the trees and lawns seemed greener and the sky bluer than I had ever seen before. The whole world appeared as if it had been cleaned. The air seemed pollutionless and clean. It was not the world that needed cleaning. The dirty film over my own soul had been peeled away. The fresh clean air of reality was sparkling wine. I had to fight an urge to giggle at absolutely nothing. Drunk! And very nearly disorderly!

I have often heard it said that those who suffer a hangover need "the hair of the dog that bit them"—in other words, a little more of whatever was drunk in excess the night before. Now I cannot say that I have ever heard of a "Holy Spirit hangover," but I can at least see something of a similarity.

Paul told the Ephesians, "And be not drunk with wine...be filled with the Spirit" (Eph. 5:18).

The Greek tense employed might more nearly (apart from its awkwardness in English) have been translated, "...be being filled." An earthier translation might read, "If you want to stay under the influence, you have to keep drinking."

A famous sculptor was once asked how, out of a shapeless formless block of granite, he could create a statue of a horse so lively that it appeared as if it might gallop away at any moment.

"It is quite easy," he replied. "I simply take my hammer and my chisels and chip away everything that does not look like a horse."

That is the ongoing work of the Holy Spirit in the life of the believer. The Holy Spirit must chip away everything that does not look like Jesus. Certainly a great deal is instantly accomplished in the moment of Holy Spirit baptism.

It must be remembered, though, that much remains to be done. The habits of holiness are important. Prayer, the constant study of the Word, praise and public worship are just the right cocktails to keep us going. Unceasing prayer is the "hidden hip flask" of a Spirit-filled Christian. From his pocket New Testament the believer can steal a "nip" between classes or a lunch break.

Some have made these habits the definition of holiness. Whether intentionally or accidentally they transmitted the message that lots of prayer and Bible study would make one holy. It simply won't do it. Devotional discipline is the lifeline of the sanctified life, but you cannot memorize enough Bible verses to cleanse your heart of bitterness, anger, and pride.

The Spirit of holiness does in us what we cannot massage in through our pores. We surrender; He sanctifies. We consecrate; He purifies. We place our lives on His altar as they are; He breathes upon them to make them what He wants them to be.

The glorious hope of holiness is that we can be changed. The evangelical world has heard so much about forgiving grace that it is doubtful if there remains even one unconvinced soul in the church world. We are blessedly assured that God will forgive us. What we need now is to believe He *will* change us—change our habits, our hearts, and our proud, self-centered arrogance.

When the seventy returned to Jerusalem bubbling with reports of miracles of healing and deliverances, Jesus responded with a cryptic reference to Satan. "And he said unto them, I beheld Satan as lightning fall from heaven" (Luke 10:18). Some say Jesus was rejoicing with them in their demonstration of the ministry of power. Perhaps. Certainly Jesus' victory over Satan is to be manifested in miracles in and through His church. In the light of the context, however, Jesus was surely making a far deeper response. Certainly the Lord was pleased with their thrilling stories of supernatural ministry. They were doing exactly what He had sent them to do. Even so, He was also reminding them that power in ministry can destroy.

> Remember, even before you were born, before the earth was old, I saw the heavenly revolt. I saw the son of the morning, the most beautiful archangel who waited before the Father's glory. I saw Lucifer. I saw him robed in a loveliness you have never imagined and endued by God with a marvelous richness and diversity of gifts. I saw him begin to take personal

> pride in the handiwork of God, to crack
> the universe at the seams. And I saw him
> fall from heaven like a bolt of lightning,
> never again to minister before God.
> —AUTHOR'S PARAPHRASE OF LUKE 10:18

Later, after the outpouring of the Holy Spirit, the apostles remembered Jesus' admonition. Far from denying their miraculous ministry of healing, deliverance, and public evangelism, they exercised it to the awe of all Jerusalem. How could they deny that remarkable morning of glorious "drunkenness?" Never! However, they were also determined not to lose their anointing through pride and ego. Christ, their humble master, their servant leader, was their model in ministry.

True holiness is the mind of Christ, and His mind is the mind of humility.

The story is told that throughout the years of bloody conflict in the American Civil War, one general made a consistent, unwavering witness of Christ to his troops and his superiors. His own commanding general, Sherman, often made light of such bold faith.

Finally when the war ended, on the eve of the victory parade down Pennsylvania Avenue,

Sherman called the general to his headquarters in Washington, DC. The president himself would review the troops as thousands cheered the triumphant armies of the North. However, that night General Sherman had sobering words for his Christian subordinate.

"My friend," Sherman began, "I am going to ask you to stand aside tomorrow and allow an associate of mine to lead your troops in the parade."

"What?" gasped the startled man.

"Yes," Sherman continued, "he was with me at West Point. He faithfully served here in Washington during the entire war, but he has no troops to lead tomorrow. He has officially asked me to give him your place. I *intend* to grant his request."

"But General Sherman," the shocked officer replied, "this is unjust. I led those men in battle. I deserve this one moment of honor."

"That is true," Sherman answered. "But you have been telling me for four years that you are a *Christian*. If you *are* a Christian, then stand aside."

"All right," the officer said. "On that basis I will gladly stand aside. As an officer, I protest, but

83

as a follower of Jesus, I will happily give up my place. Let him lead; I will ride with the enlisted men in the column."

"That's all I wanted to hear," Sherman said, with a lilt in his voice and a sudden twinkle in his eye. "Let him ride at the head of your column. You shall ride at my right hand at the head of the whole army."

We do not have to put ourselves forward. When Christ made Himself of no reputation, His Father lifted him up above all others. When we yield up our reputations as a sacrifice, He will vindicate His name, as well as those who have received the mind of Christ. When we grasp for power, jockey for position, and claim a reputation for spirituality, we totter on the brink of losing all. The one who presses angrily forward, demanding that his "prophecy" be heard, refusing to submit his "gifts" to authority, has not the mind of Christ. The very thing—the thoughts of Jesus for others—that would propel him into the spotlight will soon be soiled and useless.

Defending our reputations is a useless waste of energy. We must instead commit our promotions into God's hands. When the Word became a man, even the servant of men, God, through

Him, demonstrated His great power for healing, miracles, and gifts! The Christ of God was willing to wash feet. Let him who would be the most gifted servant of God become the most giving servant of humanity.

Have no fear that it will come to nothing. Let that be swallowed up in eternity. Rather than clutching at fleeting moments of manmade glory in the name of ministry, rest in Jesus. As we make ourselves of no reputation, He will let us stand in His glory at that day. Better an eternity in the glory that streams from the throne of the Lamb than a lifetime in the admiration of undiscerning men and women.

Holiness is not the burden of the bound. It is the blessing of the broken. Holiness is the joyful, triumphant delight of the redeemed. Holiness is not grim determination to obey the law. It is life liberated, chainless, and full of joy. Holiness is not the problem. It is the answer. Holiness is not the drab life of the bound-up legalist. Holiness, true holiness of heart and life, is the hope of a generation searching for sex in the city and hoping for little more than to be one of the survivors. Holiness is the real work of a real God in real people to grant real life.

Other Books by Mark Rutland

Launch Out Into the Deep
Behind the Glittering Mask
Streams of Mercy
God of the Valleys
Nevertheless
Dream
Power
Character Matters

For more information about Global Servants or to receive a product list of the many books, audio and video tapes, CDs, and DVDs by Mark Rutland, write, call, or go online:

Global Servants
1601 Williamsburg Square
Lakeland, FL 33803
(888) 823-8772 (Toll Free)
www.globalservants.org

The Rutland Group offers leadership and church growth consultancies and cohort educational experiences.

For more information write or call:

Global Servants
1601 Williamsburg Square
Lakeland, FL 33803
(888) 823-8772 (Toll Free)

For more information about
Southeastern University write or call:

Southeastern University
1000 Longfellow Blvd.
Lakeland, FL 33801
(863) 667-5000 (Main Number)